# I SPY
## With My Little Eye...
# Animals

Nadia Haq

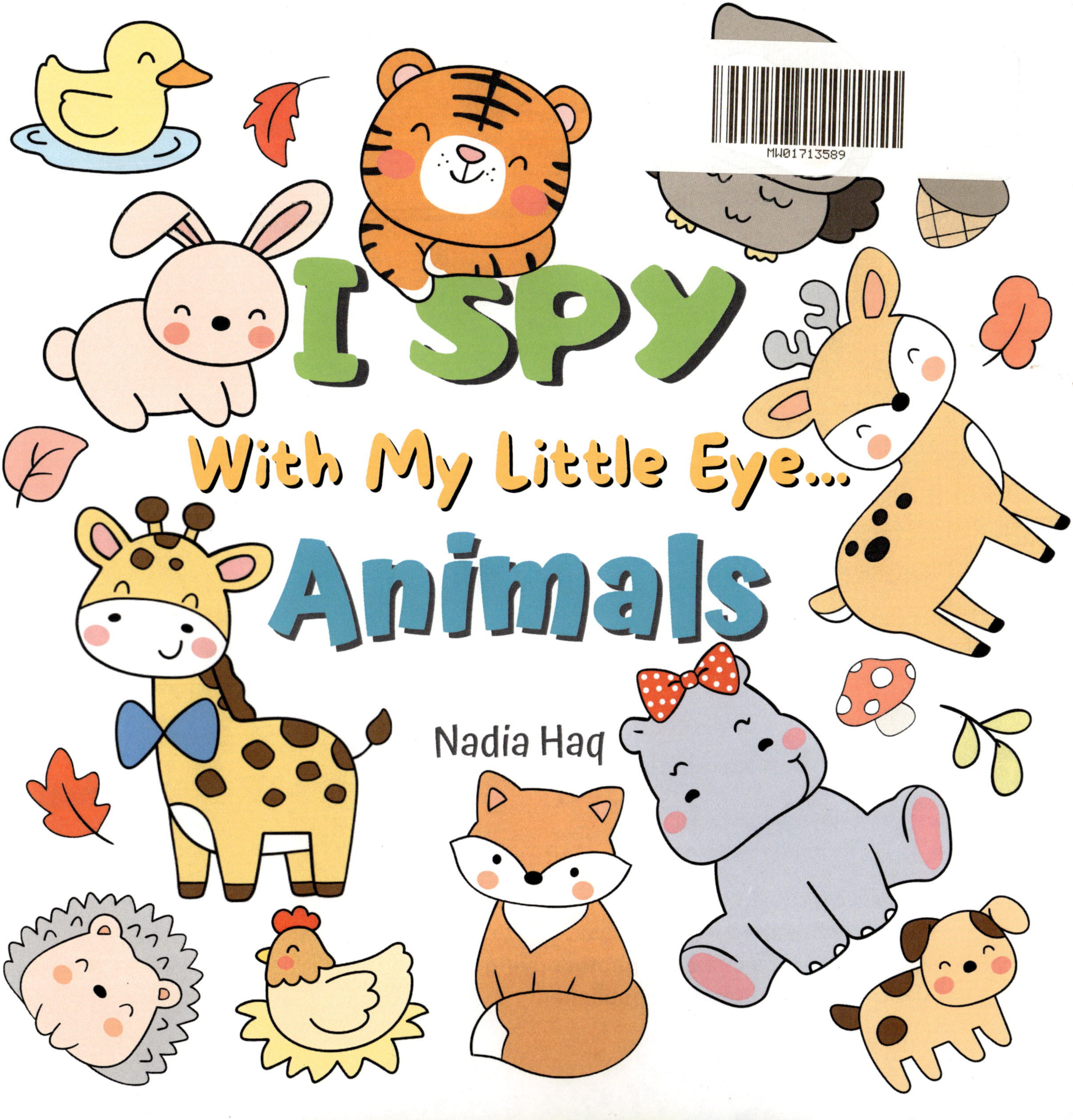

# Can you solve all the puzzles?

# This book belongs to:

# I Spy With My Little Eye
# All The
# Cats

Fun Fact: Cats can make more than 100 different vocal sounds.

# I Spy With My Little Eye All The

# Ducks

✳ Fun Fact: Ducks are social animals who feel most at ease when they're in a larger group of other ducks.

# I Spy With My Little Eye All The

# Deer

✳ Fun Fact: Deer can jump up to 10ft high.

# I Spy With My Little Eye All The Giraffes

Fun Fact: Giraffes don't need too much sleep, they only sleep between 10 minutes and 2 hours.

# I Spy With My Little Eye All The

# Owls

* Fun Fact: Owls can turn their heads almost completely around.

# I Spy With My Little Eye All The Cows

✳ Fun Fact: Cows are colorblind to red and green colors.

# I Spy With My Little Eye All The

# Rabbits

✳ Fun Fact: A rabbit's teeth never stop growing! By chewing on grasses, wildflowers, and vegetables, they keep their teeth short.

# I Spy With My Little Eye All The

# Tigers

*Fun Fact: Tigers have stripes on their skin, not just the fur.

# I Spy With My Little Eye All The

# Raccoons

✳ Fun Fact: Raccoons are nocturnal animals. They are awake during the night and sleep all day.

# I Spy With My Little Eye All The

# Horses

✳ Fun Fact: Horses can sleep standing up and lying down.

# I Spy With My Little Eye All The Monkeys

✳ Fun Fact: Monkeys have unique fingerprints like humans.

# I Spy With My Little Eye All The

# Hedgehogs

✳ Fun Fact: Hedgehogs have around 5000 to 7000 spines.

# I Spy With My Little Eye All The Bears

Fun Fact: Bears are related to walruses, seals, and sea lions.

# I Spy With My Little Eye All The

# Pigs

Fun Fact: Pigs love to roll in the mud because it keeps them cool.

# I Spy With My Little Eye All The

# Dogs

✳ Fun Fact: Dogs' noses are 1000 times more sensitive than ours.

# I Spy With My Little Eye All The

# Foxes

Fun Fact: Foxes have whiskers on their legs as well as around their faces, which they use to help them find their way.

# Answers

=7

=5

=10

=4

=6

=9

=8

=3

# Answers

=2

=1

=4

=9

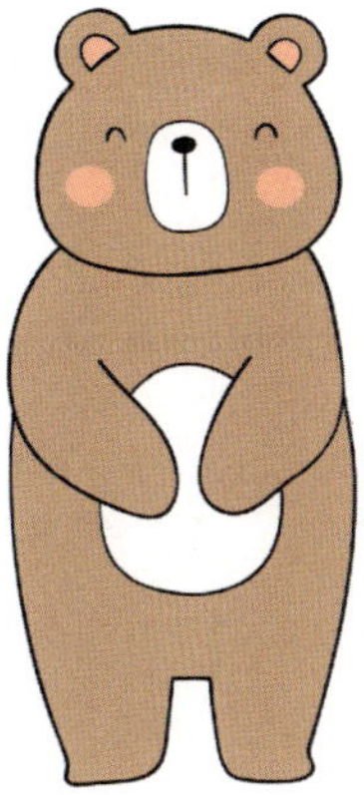

=3

=5

=7

=8

Enjoying this I Spy With My Little Eye Animals book?

We would appreciate it if you could please leave us a review. We value your feedback to help improve our books.

Thank you for your support.

You are amazing.

Manufactured by Amazon.ca
Bolton, ON

30446328R00024